THE THREE DEMIGODS, THE FIVE EMPERORS AND THE CHINESE DRAGON

MYTHOLOGY 4TH GRADE
CHILDREN'S FOLK TALES & MYTHS

Speedy Publishing LLC

40 E. Main St. #1156

Newark, DE 19711

www.speedypublishing.com

Copyright 2017

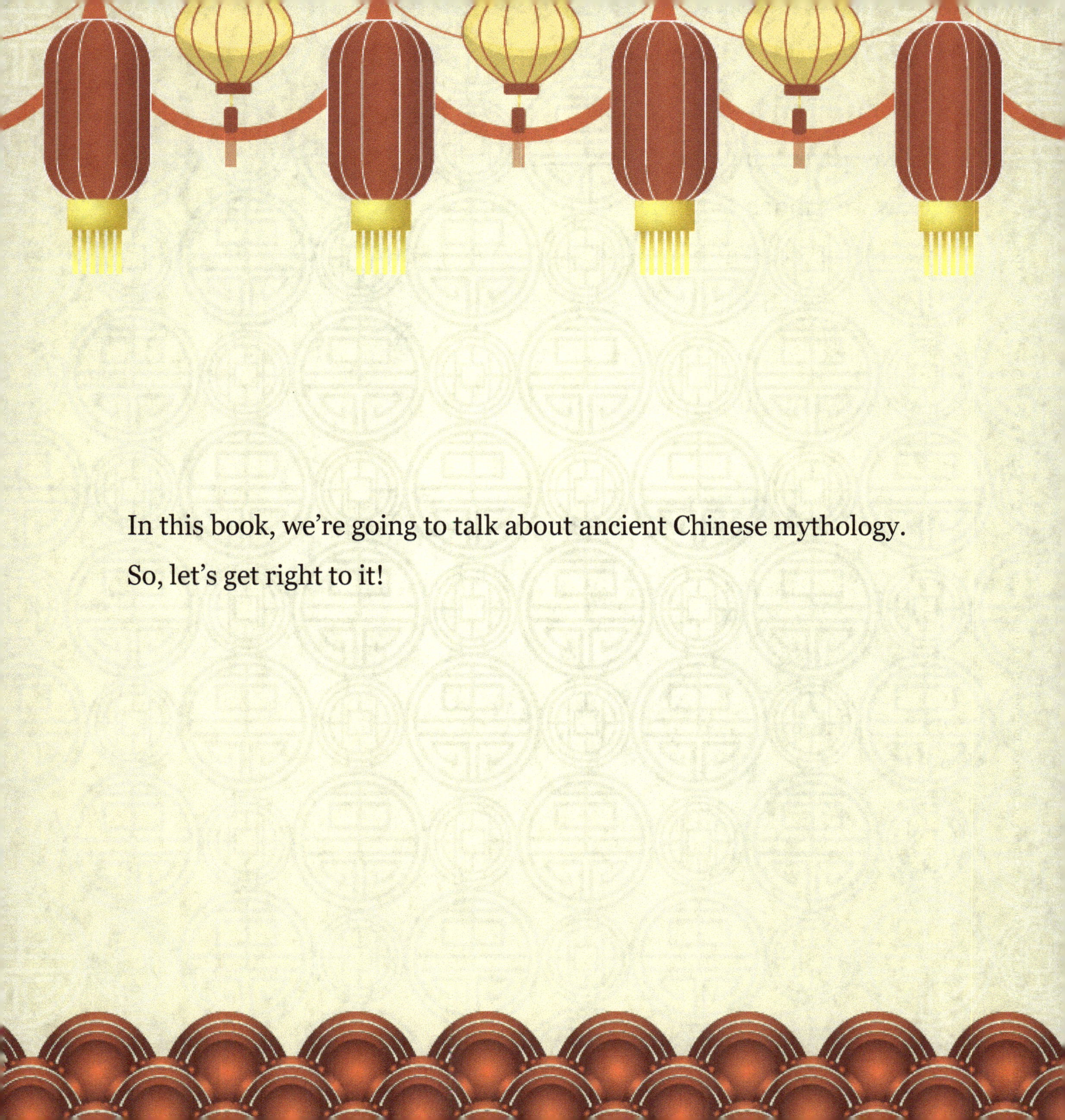

In this book, we're going to talk about ancient Chinese mythology.

So, let's get right to it!

The civilization of China began in the Yellow River Valley over 5,000 years ago. However, much of China's early history wasn't recorded until 200 BC. Today we don't know whether these early histories were based on actual events or whether they were mythology or a combination of both.

YELLOW RIVER

Even if they are not based on historical fact, they are still very important, because they were powerful stories that formed the basis of all Chinese culture. The stories of the Three Demigods and the Five Emperors provided guidelines for how to live life and for the values that became important to the Chinese people.

In this account of the history, there were Three Demigods, who were also called the Three Sovereigns or the Three Sage Kings. They were:

Fu Xi

Shen Nong

Suiren

SHENNONG

TOMB OF EMPEROR HUANGDI

After the reigns of these three spiritual masters, the reign of the emperors began. The first Five Emperors, also called the Five Legendary Leaders, were:

Huangdi

Zhuanxu

Diku

Yao

Shun

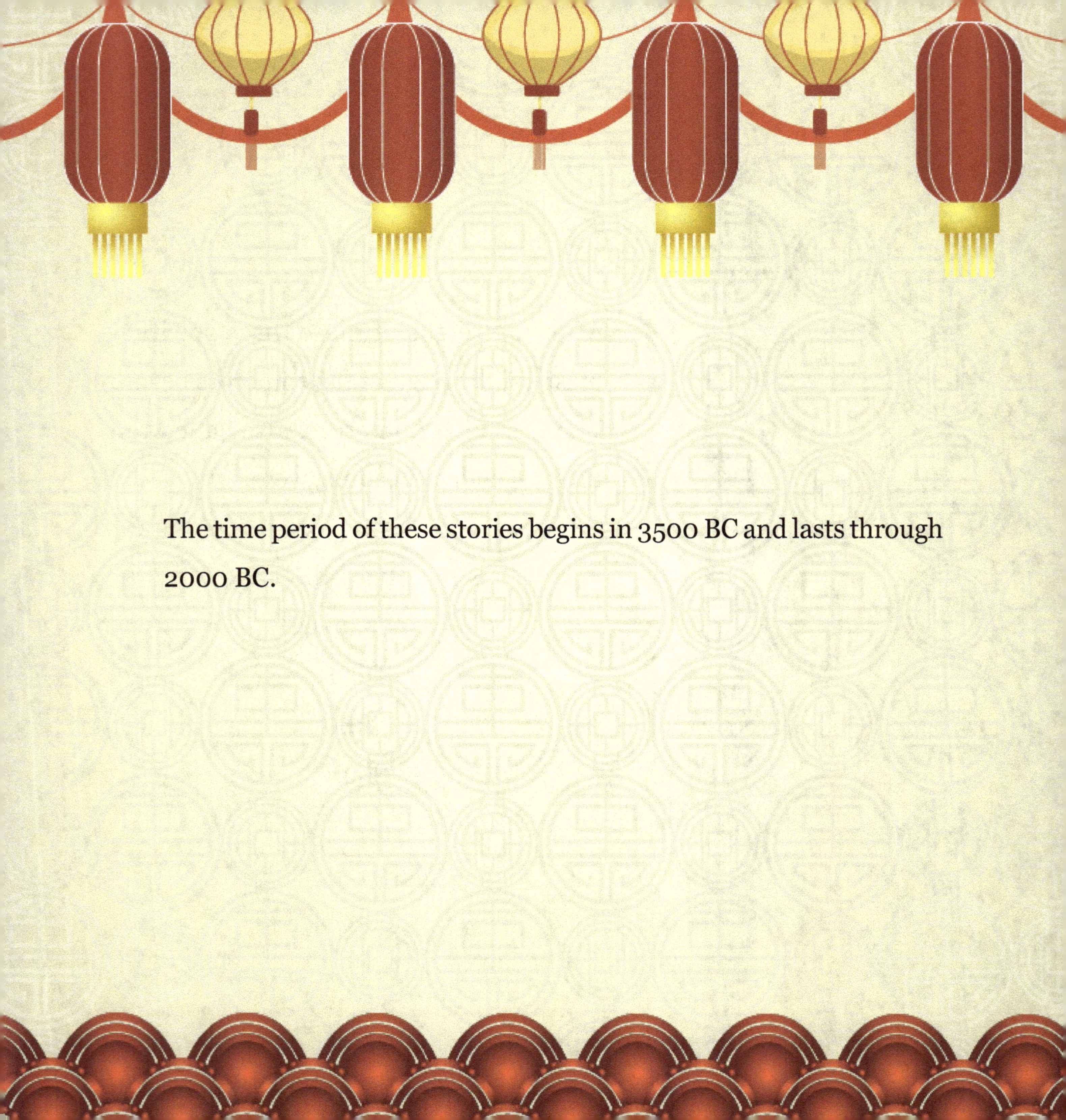

The time period of these stories begins in 3500 BC and lasts through 2000 BC.

KANGXI EMPEROR AIXIN-JUELUO XUANYE

FU XI

The first demigod was Fu Xi. He was a legendary chieftain. He taught the first people the skills of hunting and fishing. He also taught them how to breed livestock to use for food. He created the eight trigrams.

A trigram is a group of three written elements, such as three letters, three syllables, or three words. The eight trigrams are considered to be the eight gates to the greater world. They are arranged in an octagon and represent heaven, the wind, water, the mountain, the earth, the thunder, fire, and the valley.

EIGHT TRIGRAM PAVILION

FU XI

The legend states that Fu Xi went on an epic quest. He wanted to study every thing that existed both in heaven and on earth. On his quest, he saw many things but at one point he studied a river dragon. In some interpretations of the story, it was a tortoise. The creature had a series of unusual markings on its shell. These markings gave Fu Xi the idea for the trigrams.

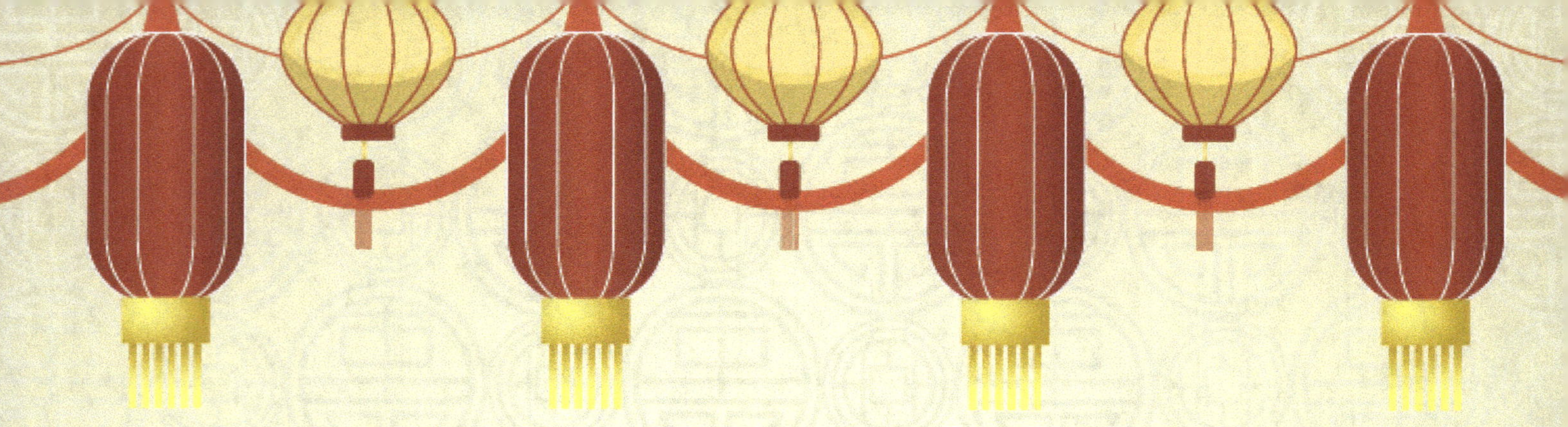

These trigrams became the basis for hexagrams, which were groups of six symbols. The I Ching, which is one of the most important ancient Chinese spiritual books, is made up of 64 hexagrams with different important meanings. The trigrams and hexagrams are used for many different patterns of associations for the seasons, directions, forces, and changes.

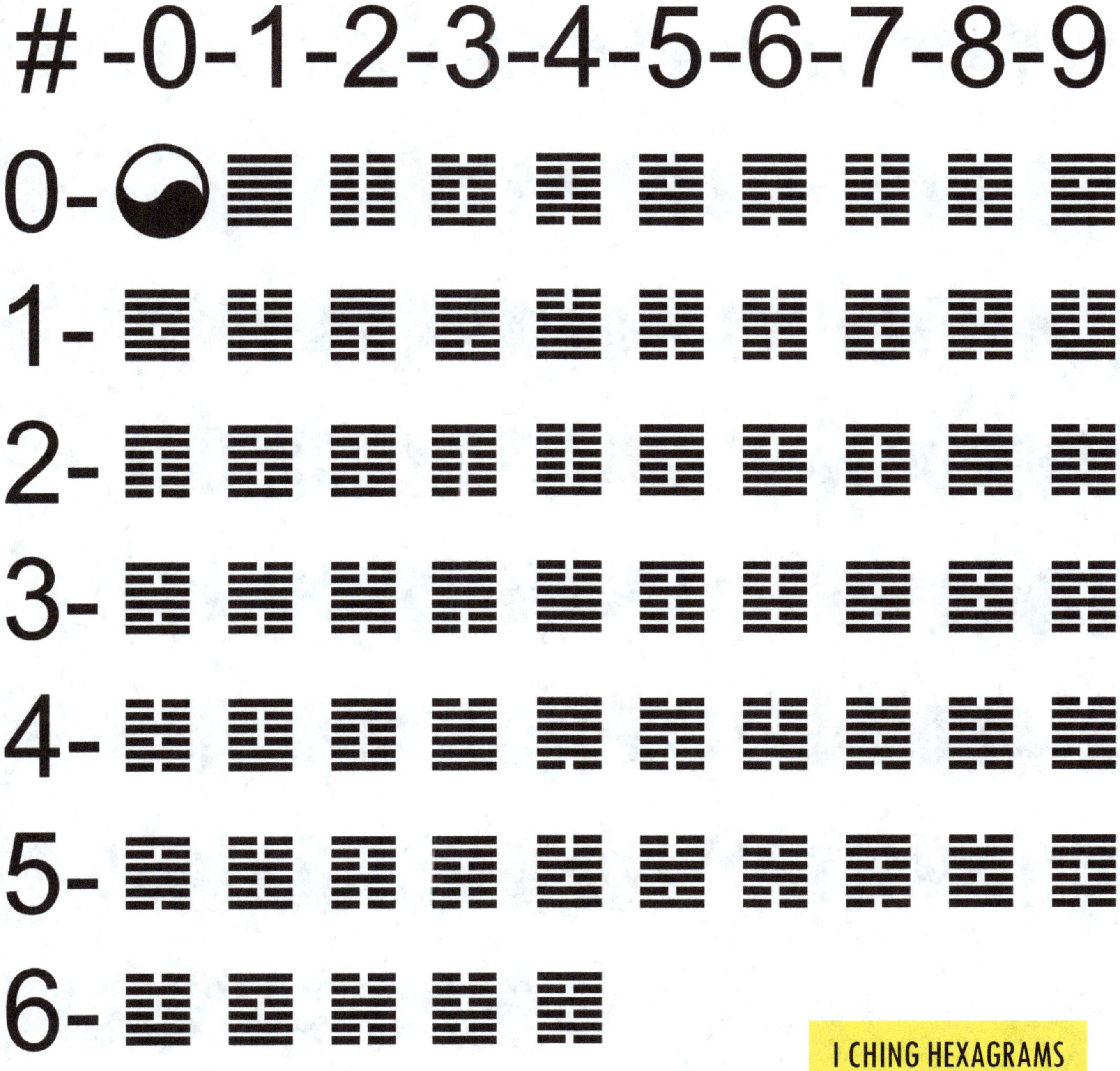

-0-1-2-3-4-5-6-7-8-9

0-

1-

2-

3-

4-

5-

6-

NUWA

In some of the stories about Fu Xi, there is a woman by the name of Nü Wa. Sometimes she is described as his sister and sometimes she's his wife. There are many stories about Nü Wa. In one story, she wandered all over the beautiful Earth by herself. She felt very lonely so she mixed soil and water to make some mud. Then, she used the mud to make people who looked like her so they would keep her company.

SHEN NONG

The second demigod was Shen Nong. His name means "spirit farmer." Shen Nong was the master of farming and he created the very first plow for people to use to till the soil. He established the first markets and he taught the people how to barter and trade with one another so they could get the things they needed. He also studied everything about plants and discovered how to use them for healing. In some of the later stories, he was the demigod who discovered how to brew tea leaves to make tea.

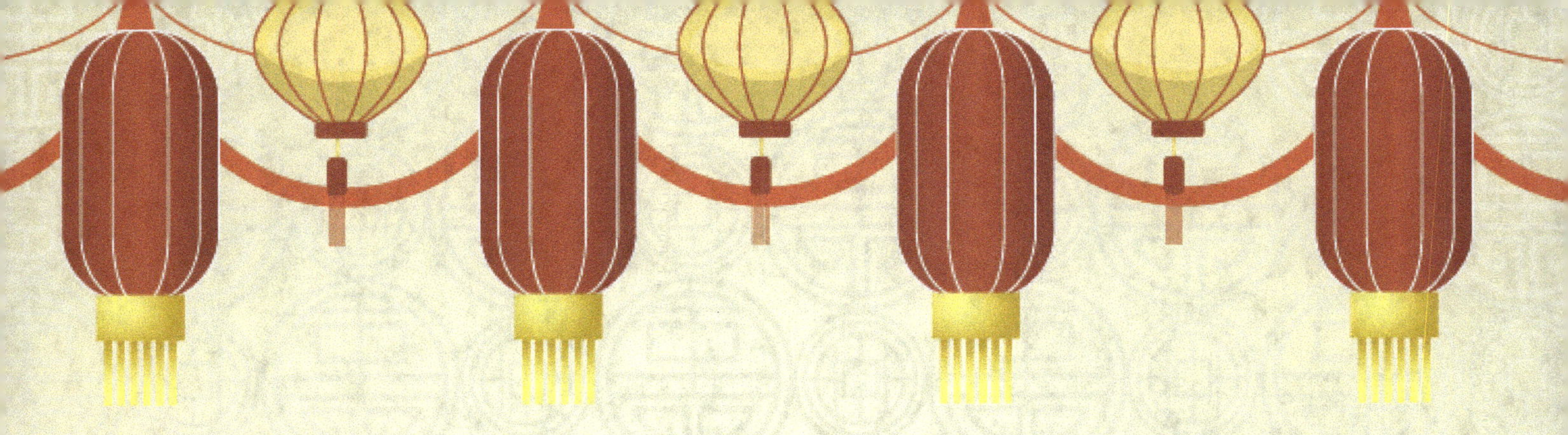

SUIREN

The third demigod was Suiren. He was the one who made the important discovery of fire for mankind to use. The story says that he had heard of a tree in a western forest that was bright like the sun.

When Suiren found the tree, he noticed that there were many woodpeckers hitting the trunk with their beaks. When they did this, sparks flew. He watched what they were doing and he learned to rub two sticks together to start a fire. Once he mastered fire, he taught the Chinese people how to use it to stay warm and also how to cook their meat over fire so they wouldn't get sick.

HUANGDI STELE IN THE SACRIFICIAL HALL OF THE XUANYUAN TEMPLE

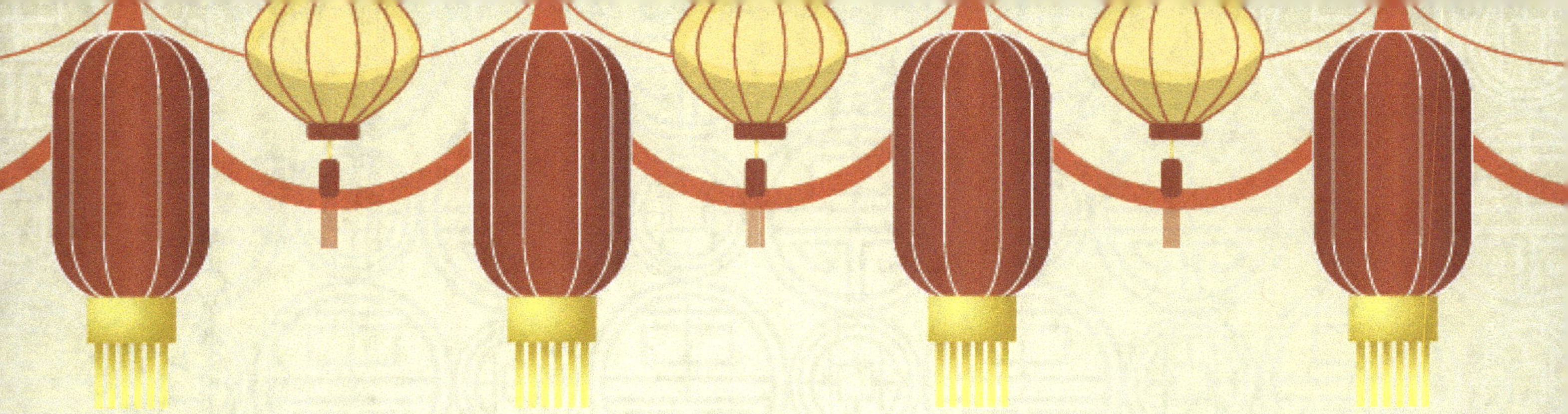

HUANGDI

The first emperor was Huangdi. He was also called the Yellow Emperor. He reigned eight generations after the second demigod Shen Nong. He overthrew an evil king and many powerful leaders pledged their loyalty to him as a result. He was able to rule for a hundred years although he had to fight many wars with invaders.

Huangdi was an ideal leader in many ways. He knew how to bring together talented people with many different backgrounds. These people shared their creativity and intelligence to develop the principles of mathematics as well as astronomy. They established the Chinese calendar and they also invented a writing system and a legal code. They invented new construction methods and tools for measurement. They even invented the scales of music.

A BRONZE ASTRONOMICAL INSTRUMENT
J. Child
1875.

YELLOW EMPEROR

The oldest medical text in China was written from conversations that the emperor had with his doctor on how to treat and prevent diseases. One of the emperor's wives, Lei Zu, created the way to use silk from silk worms to make cloth.

ZHUANXU

The second emperor was Zhuanxu and he was one of Huangdi's grandsons. He made contributions to the Chinese calendar as well as to the practice of astrology. He is also credited for composing one of the first pieces of music called "The Answer to the Clouds."

CHINESE ASTROLOGY SYMBOLS

DIKU

The third emperor was Diku and he was one of Huangdi's great grandsons. It was said that in the seasons of spring and summer, Diku rode a dragon and in the fall and in the winter, he rode a horse. He invented many types of musical instruments and composed beautiful songs.

YAO

The fourth emperor was Yao. One of his strengths was to get different clans to work together. He created harmony among the villagers in different cities. He was known for beginning by establishing virtue in himself and then extending his virtue to the world. Although he received the right to rule from his father, he is largely remembered for how he decided who would rule after him.

EMPEROR YAO

EMPEROR YAO STATUE

He felt his own son wasn't capable of being a ruler, so he selected a young man called Shun who he thought was virtuous. He mentored Shun for thirty years and gave him progressively more difficult tasks until Shun was ready to rule. Shun had shown that he could handle challenging political situations.

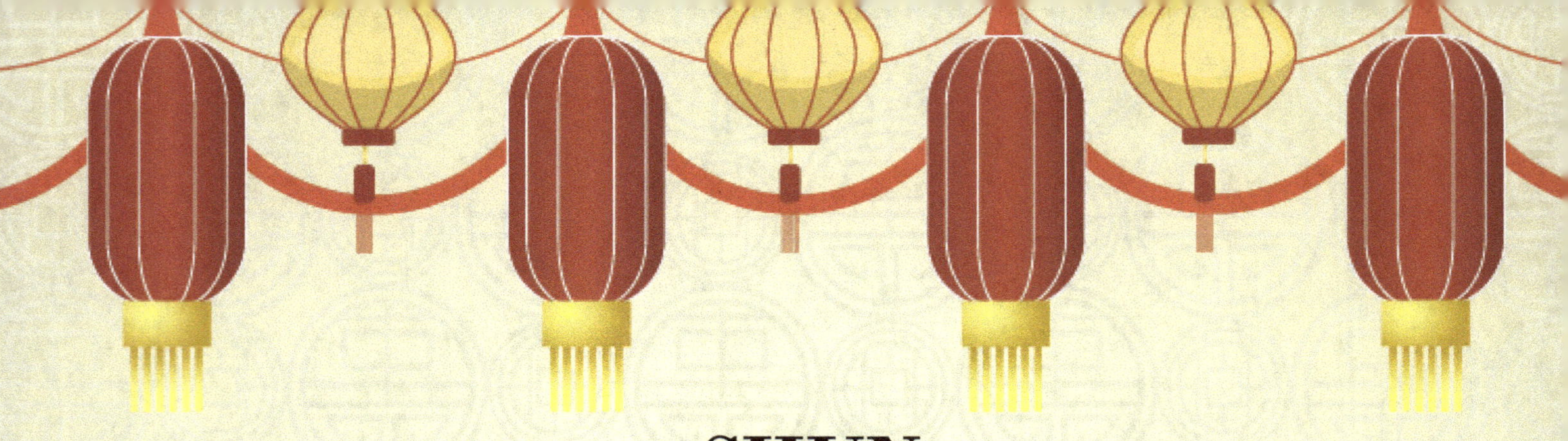

SHUN

The fifth emperor was Shun. Thanks to the help from his mentor, Yao, Shun was ready to take over the position of emperor. Some people in China didn't want to follow the lifestyle of farmers and they caused unrest among the other people. Shun sent these barbarians out to remote areas so that they wouldn't disturb the other people who were living in harmony. He gave authority to people who had the interest of the public at heart. He promoted empathetic and wise people to help him rule the kingdom.

EMPEROR SHUN

One of the famous stories about Shun tells how he managed problems within his kingdom. There was a village of farmers who were fighting over their lands. Shun disguised himself and went to live there as a farmer. After a year, all the fighting stopped.

There was a village of fishermen who were fighting over who could fish from different sections of a riverbank. Shun disguised himself again and went to live there for a year. At the end of a year's time, the quarreling stopped, and they had begun a system of sharing their rights.

Finally, there was a village of men who made pottery, but it wasn't of good quality. Their pottery wasn't shaped well. Shun disguised himself and pretended he was a potter. In a short time, the pottery was some of the most beautiful and most useful in the entire land.

Shun had very good control over his own emotions. He was the son of a man who was both blind and stupid. His mother was dishonest and his half brother was very arrogant. Somehow, Shun maintained a virtuous life, and didn't become wicked even though he was around wicked people.

EMPEROR SHUN PERFORMS DIVINATION IN THE PALACE

THE SYMBOL OF
THE DRAGON

In Chinese mythology, the dragon appears frequently. Dragons are sometimes depicted as long creatures with four legs that have bodies that look like snakes. They have powerful jaws and sometimes they have wings. All dragons can fly and they are able to control the weather, even dangerous weather like thunderstorms and tornadoes.

The emperor used the powerful dragon as his symbol and only he could wear robes that had a dragon design. Legend says that the Yellow Emperor changed into a dragon and ascended into heaven when he passed away.

CHINESE SUMMER COURT ROBE

WHAT COMPOSED CHINA'S RICH HISTORY...

The history of ancient China is composed of mythological stories of three demigods and five emperors. These wise rulers formed the culture of China. Although no one knows if they were real or not, their stories were powerful and shaped the values of the Chinese people and the way they lived their lives.

Awesome! Now that you've read about ancient Chinese mythology, you may want to read more about Chinese art in the Baby Professor book The Three Perfections of Ancient China Art.

Visit
BABY PROFESSOR
EDUCATION KIDS
www.BabyProfessorBooks.com
to download Free Baby Professor eBooks
and view our catalog of new and exciting
Children's Books